Kim and Sam

by Tristan Horrom
illustrated by Nicole In Den Bosch

Decodable 11

Mc Graw Hill Education

Bothell, WA • Chicago, IL • Columbus, OH • New York, NY

MHEonline.com

Send all inquiries to:
McGraw-Hill Education
8787 Orion Place
Columbus, OH 43240

ISBN: 978-0-02-145271-2
MHID: 0-02-145271-7

Printed in China

9 10 11 12 13 DSS 28 27 26 25 24

Kim and Sam look at a plan.

We can run with a wind.

Kim and Sam can win!

We can run it up.

Look at Kim and Sam!

Kim can go fast with Sam!